From Pink to Blue

An Enlightening Concept That Awakens
"Truth of Being" and Reminds You To
Focus On The Path That You
Were Born To Follow.

Marilyn Louise Lawrence

BALBOA.
PRESS

A DIVISION OF HAY HOUSE

ISBN: 978-1-4525-5238-5 (sc)
ISBN: 978-1-4525-5237-8 (e)

Library of Congress Control Number: 2012908954

Balboa Press books may be ordered through booksellers or by contacting:

Balboa Press
A Division of Hay House
1663 Liberty Drive
Bloomington, IN 47403
www.balboapress.com
1-(877) 407-4847

Because of the dynamic nature of the Internet, any web addresses or
links contained in this book may have changed since publication and may
no longer be valid. The views expressed in this work are solely those
of the author and do not necessarily reflect the views of the publisher,
and the publisher hereby disclaims any responsibility for them.

The author of this book does not dispense medical advice or prescribe the
use of any technique as a form of treatment for physical, emotional, or medical
problems without the advice of a physician, either directly or indirectly. The
intent of the author is only to offer information of a general nature to help
you in your quest for emotional and spiritual well-being. In the event you use
any of the information in this book for yourself, which is your constitutional
right, the author and the publisher assume no responsibility for your actions.

Any people depicted in stock imagery provided by Thinkstock are models,
and such images are being used for illustrative purposes only.
Certain stock imagery © Thinkstock.

Printed in the United States of America
Balboa Press rev. date: 06/27/12

I lovingly thank

God, The Angels and my Guides for trusting me
with this concept and these words to share.

Krystal Hafeman Sause,
for reminding me of the light and giving me
constant, unwavering
love and support.

Jacki Williams McCormack,
for reminding me "What I do Matters".

Debbie McOmie Leader,
for suggesting this book is a
"mandatory read".

My husband and soul-mate Dale

My son Michael, who is my brilliant and
logical sounding board and critique.

Contents

Preface

The following is a
collaboration of opinions and ideas.
Mine, gathered through observing my son and
nieces grow, through interviews with children
and observations of the same, along with
messages that were given to me as I wrote.
It is by means of these observations
and messages that guided me to a
profound Awareness, thus Knowingness.

This Knowingness
lead to an important
Concept.

A Concept
that I was asked to share for the purpose of
raising universal consciousness.

During the research period for my book,
I had the honor of spending time and
interviewing a few children. I had
pre-determined questions that I asked of each of
the children and then asked them to expand on any
of the questions they had ideas about or wanted
to discuss more. As each child became more
comfortable with the process, they
answered my questions and shared with
me personal situations, some of which
triggered an emotional response as they recounted
experiences that lead to changes in their
lives, the changes of their own ideas,
aspirations and colors. All of these
interviews demonstrated changes that were made not
because of the individual's desires,
but because of the
influence of another or others.

Thank you to the following children for sharing
their thoughts, ideas, and memories with me:

Elizabeth McIsaac
Daniel McCormack
Maile McCormack
Mitchell McCormack
Marin McCormack
Jade Stowell
Kendall Stowell

Chapter One

Awareness
To
Knowingness

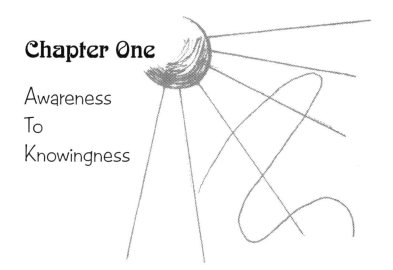

As I sat watching one of my nieces twirl herself around the living room clad with a towel as a cape and a spatula as a wand, I was reminded of years past as I watched other nieces, now beautiful grown women, delight themselves in the adventures of infinite possibilities. Consumed so deeply with the vision of limitless realms, they were unaware of anyone or anything. Pure natural belief illuminated from them. Belief that each of us is born with, the belief that we can be anything we want to be, including a princess in a beautifully adorned gown with a magical wand, dancing in near perfect step as the music floats through the air, in our ears, for only us to hear.

I smile when I think of my own son at age 3 walking down the stairs of our home wearing only a cowboy hat, cowboy boots and a holster, fast on the trail of something that his imagination deemed worthy of a chase. Knar did I ever stop his search, with the exception of adding clothing to the mix.

I have such fond memories as I think about their childhoods and feel so fortunate to have witnessed their "bright light" the times I was able. Certainly each differs in personality, actions, emotions, but there is and was one constant in all of their young lives, an unwavering faith that they were special. It is that Faith that is given to each child, rather "gifted" to each child, whether boy or girl when they enter this world.

Each child had a favorite color at this young age; pink was the first choice of most of my nieces, a pure woman's energy color. Each thought themselves to be the perfect image of their imagination.

What a wonderful thing to witness and enjoy.

However, something happens to children I have observed, by the time they near the age of seven to eight. Their sense of personal image is shaken and sometimes completely tumbled. Something has happened to the Faith in infinite possibilities that was gifted to them. In this wavering of character, their favorite things change. Whether that is what they want to be when they grow up, to their favorite color, things change, sometimes slowly, sometimes it seems overnight.

There is a change, as I observed just recently in my niece, a change in favorite color from pink to blue.

Girls no longer like princesses, or think they are or can be one. A towel could certainly never be a gown. Being called a princess has changed from a delight to an insult of sort.

Boys, who once delighted themselves stomping around the house in the most perfect self-appointed example of a dinosaur, complete with snarls and roars, find the idea silly. Being a real cowboy by simply wearing boats and a hat is not logical or possible.

"Children must be taught how to think, not what to think". Margaret Mead

Yes, their image of themselves, the image that was gifted to them from God, which they delighted in for all their young lives, was now challenged. Self-doubt and judging takes the place of pure faith and limitless possibilities. Whether this comes from older children, mothers, fathers, grandparents, aunts, uncles, somewhere, someone has interrupted their own natural flow. Someone has penetrated their very core of right and wrong and made these children question themselves. They are told that there is no such thing as princesses and magical lands, lest grow up to be a princess. They are ridiculed and laughed at, made fun of and teased. The beautiful child that once floated with infinite possibilities is changed, their spirit deflated, corrupted in a sense, and they can never go back. This child will now question everything that he or she thought to be true and right in their informative years. They now doubt their own choices.

What a sad thing we have done. What a wrong has been committed.

Now they are faced with the task of relearning things, however this time to someone else's steps. They are confused and non-committal fearing ridicule. The simplest task may seem difficult, they struggle to make sense of things, often times masking their behavior with forgetfulness or humor.

The confusion is not because they do not know the information or cannot learn it; the confusion is not because they are unable to make simple decisions. It is instead because they are afraid of being wrong, being in trouble.

The fact that everything they thought to be true in their younger lives has been judged by a party of their peers or superiors, judged, criticized and more times than not corrected, they have been placed in the position of doubting everything they think is right.

These children have been forced to be someone they are not and for that, they are placed in the position of questioning everything.

They have to again "figure things out," as told to me by one of the children I interviewed.

Children are placed in the position of relearning nearly everything. What is acceptable behavior, answers, personality, likes, dislikes, relearning everything based not on them, but based on other people or society. They have been taught doubt, doubt in themselves.

Having been so deeply saddened when this process was made aware to me and realizing this process has and would repeat itself generation after generation, I knew it was time to share this Awareness-Knowingness-Concept.

"If you want your children to be intelligent, read them fairy tales. If you want them to be more intelligent, read them more fairy tales". Albert Einstein

Chapter Two

A Pattern leading to The "Concept"

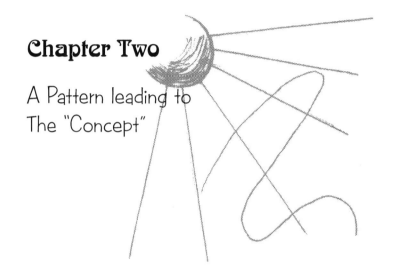

It is the Concept of telling a child that they cannot be their dream, that their ideas and opinions are wrong or silly that needs to be addressed; it needs to be modified for the betterment of our children's future, for everyone's future really.

If we allow every child to believe in their dreams, then their "purpose" will never be doubted. If their purpose is never doubted, then achieving their "greatest good" will happen seamlessly.

Instead of spending years correcting the harm of hiding their inner truths, they will spend those years in their "greatest good", achieving more than could even be imagined I would venture to say.

"There is no greater insight into the future than recognizing...when we save our children, we save ourselves". Margaret Mead

As it is now, it is not until later in life, sometimes much later in life and sadly, sometimes never, that many women and men again begin to embrace their truth of infinite possibilities. Women and men spend hours, rather years searching, studying and processing. Through long painful analyzing and letting go of past violations that have been stored deeply inside, below piles of memories, each having to be peeled away, examined, addressed and released.

I think it is important at this point to recognize that not all children have been raised to doubt themselves and their unique purpose for life.

They have been spared the pain of self-doubt. Kudos to those adults, whoever you are, for having the insight to give complete and constant unconditional love without judgment and ridicule. I commend you for realizing the importance of the role you have taken in aiding in the development of young souls. That knowing for every action there is a reaction and with full consciousness making choices to help develop the young souls that were blessed to be around you.

I am hoping with the words combined here in these pages to open the minds of some who had never had the opportunity to realize that their actions were affecting others in a negative way. In effect striping away the individual character given to that child. "People do not know what they do not know" I always say.

Unless something is brought to someone's attention, no changes would be made, no changes thought necessary and they would walk in the same path, continuing the same process of removing individual personalities, of dowsing the light on a golden soul.

Another conversation is brought to mind now. I heard someone say, every child needs someone to tease them and bully them when they are little, it makes them tough.

Yes, unfortunately it does do just that. It teaches children at a young age that they need to protect themselves and put up walls; that people will be out to cut them down. Just the opposite of what I am striving to accomplish. Joking, laughing and humor create joy and is essential, however not at the expense of another's good. I am suggesting behaviors that will shift the whole conscious energy in the world to one of Enlightenment, "Truth of Being" and divinely guided purpose. Imagine the deep satisfaction and joy that will be felt in doing so and then imagine that energy being spread and multiplied. Manifestations in accomplishments and developments would be limitless!

> "Rebel children, I urge you, fight the turgid
> slick of conformity with which they seek
> to smother your glory". Russell Brand

I was speaking with my now adult son about this subject, telling him that I felt very strongly about this. I told him that you never hear parents telling their sons that they cannot be a firefighter or police officer as they run through the house playing "cops and robbers"; however, you do hear adults telling little girls that they cannot be princesses. He remarked, "that was because there is no such thing as princesses".

My work was cut out for me. My own son had forgotten the possibilities of chasing bad guys clad in his Spiderman suit.

It is the concept that I am trying to bring to attention. If you instill self-doubt in children at their young informative ages then we are directly affecting their self-propelled drive to be and do anything in the world. To grasp whatever it is that they truly believe in and pursue it without fear of judgment and criticism and teasing. If left alone little girls will realize on their own the likelihood of being a princess and will find their own purpose without second-guessing their drive and decision. I believe strongly that we need to be the best mentors we can be for these little souls.

That means not teasing them for wanting to be whatever makes them happy at the time, but rejoicing with them and teaching them that anything in this world is possible.

What a world we would create if we had children with pure and unlimited intention focusing on the path that was designed for them.

I know that there will be some that say "but this ...or but that"; please remember the "Concept" I am talking about; a process of enlightened communication.

"You think the only people who are people,
are the people who look and think like you.
But if you walk the footsteps of a stranger,
you'll learn things you never knew you never
knew". Pocahontas. Walt Disney Company

Every child is a gift from God, a bright light
with a special purpose for their life.

It is our job to stop getting in the way.

It is our job to be wise enough

To Guide
without directing.

To Teach
without destroying.

To Protect
without preventing.

To Provide for
without controlling.

To Recognize
and
Nurture
the very essence of their being.

It is like the bumpers on the walls of the bumper car game at a fair or amusement park. The bumpers bounce the cars back in to the game, each car is operated by its own driver, with their own agenda; the bumpers just help keep the cars in the game.

So too is it our job to keep these children "in the game", in "their game". To help bounce them back when they lose control or focus and to allow them to be their own driver, respecting in the fact that they are on their own journey in life.

The easiest way to start is to (please) stop teasing, belittling and creating self-doubt. Instead, rejoice in the observation of limitless imagination and possibilities. Who knows, it may just help you start recognizing your own journey and help you fill yourself with the joy of your own divine grace.

At birth adults need to begin saying, "I believe and support your purpose". Teach others around them, including other children to say the same thing. When you hear a child being teased or ridiculed assume the role of enlightener by teaching the importance of protecting individuals own paths.

If we all work together, helping each other, uniting in the cause of greatness of purpose, then we will start a new trend. WE will create a shift in society. Just like with anything, it needs to start somewhere with someone, make that someone you.

"I believe in you and support you and your life purpose".

"Accept children the way we accept trees- with gratitude, because they are a blessing- but do not have expectations or desires. You don't expect trees to change; you love them as they are". Isabel Allende

Create your own higher awareness to what your words and actions are doing and have done.

Pay very close attention to your reactions to your children's words and behaviors.

When you create this higher awareness in yourself, you will begin recognizing when you are intervening on another's life path.

Let me interject here by saying that I am not suggesting that children are allowed to misbehave and run rampant.

Allowing a child to embrace his or her own individual character and purpose is the goal. Realizing that each child has a purpose that may be completely different from that of their immediate surroundings, family, peers and still nurturing that child is the goal.

"Children aren't coloring books. You don't get to fill them with your favorite colors" Khaled Hosseini

Chapter Three

Focusing on Children Enlightens Us

I had written the prior pages and asked a couple of my friends to read the beginnings of my new book, testing the subject matter so to speak.

The most amazing thing happened. I did receive the acknowledgement I wanted regarding the importance of the concept I was sharing, but to my surprise, these women, each accomplished in their own right, were profoundly moved by the words they read. Without exception, the initial reaction was not of how their actions had or would affect that of their children or children around them, but how they were living testament of how the process had worked for, or rather against them as a child. Each of these accomplished women seemed to wilt as they shared with me stories about how their father, mother, aunt, uncle or whoever devalued them. Stories so painful to remember it brought tears to their eyes. It is a violation in sense, not one that is chargeable, but one that has lasting effects nonetheless.

Because of these honest, candid reactions, I vowed determination to spread my thoughts through words to as many as would read and listen. It was too, because of these admissions that I looked at my own life with clearer eyes. Yes, I too had been stripped of "me" as a child.

"It is never too late to have a happy childhood".
Tom Robbins, Still Life With Woodpecker"

I remember standing in front of the TV in my grandparent's living room, not more than 3 or 4 years old dancing to the songs drifting from the Ed Sullivan show as my grandmother smiled on, "beautiful merry sunshine", she would say. "Merry Sunshine" was the name my grandmother called me. It always brought warmth to my heart when she used that term of endearment towards me.

In fact, to this day I am still warmed with the unconditional joy my grandparents showered on me. I miss them all dearly.

I was raised on a farm in a community of 500. I now feel fortunate for the experiences that were taught me by this humble life and beginning. I now understand that it was me that made the choice to experience this beginning and it could be or rather was this experience that aided me in recognizing the treatment of the youths around me, knowing of their lost years and potential because of the treatment.

I do not blame anyone, I do not judge anyone, but certainly, those are things that I had to learn again. Children are not born with judgment, blame, doubt, failure; it is something that is taught to them. By the words they hear daily around them or to them. These words are spoken innocently in most cases from people unaware of the repercussions each word will generate.

As a young child, I learned if I did not talk, if I did not share my opinions and views, I would not be judged as easily. My ideas on most everything differed from that of my families, or so it seemed at the time.

So much so there were times I remember wondering if I was adopted. That thought makes me laugh now knowing that it was with intention that I belonged where I was. It has been a journey for me to make it back to my starting place. To look for and recognize my life purpose. I say starting place because that is where we are placed as children, at our starting point and then we go from there to accomplish our life's purpose. This is the basis for my message, aka Concept in this book. If people did not spend so much of their life off the track of their true-life purpose, then dreams of accomplishments will be shadowed by the actual event I would venture to say.

The idea of a world without judgment is worth the journey of realization in itself. The idea of a world filled with spiritual beings enlightened with their true potential with no doubt or invalidation takes the mind on a magical journey of wonderment. Imagine the possibilities.

I was like so many children; it seemed in school I had a difficult time trying to fit in. Trying to make myself change so that I could be like others, so they would like me.

Remembering the lesson I had learned as a child that my true views and opinions were wrong according to others; I spent my time trying to act like someone else. And guess what? I forgot me. In fact, I never really knew me, since I had spent so many years trying not to be me. I was so far away from my life's purpose because I was so far away from the true me. I now realized, with a thud, that I too became an example for my book. It was the beautiful children around me that reminded me of my path and made me realize that my path is so like that of many children.

Born with a golden light, but not being able to see it or focus on it because of the glare of others words.

A vicious circle had begun many years ago. Children redirected from their life path by people who were redirected from their own.

When I think of my mother's life, I am saddened by her wasted potential, by her distraction of purpose and her doubt to make it possible... She too was an example of the redirection. My mother was a very intelligent woman with hopes of becoming a doctor and had one of the best dry wits I, to this day, have met. Her potential was limitless, but not recognized or developed. Instead repressed.

She spent the first 7 years of her life being raised in a different state by her grandmother since her own mother was very ill. A stern grandmother who was raised in the time of proper etiquette and with a philosophy that children were to be seen and not heard. There in itself is an example of a prolonged period in history when most every child was stifled. Not given the opportunity to use their own voice or dream, but taught that of society accepted behavior.

My father's life was much the same in regards to stifling an independent spirit. I am sure if you examine your own life and that of your parents, cousins, friends, etc. you will find the same pattern. A pattern of expected uniformity. I liken it to a row of worker ants. Following the same path, doing the same thing, with no originality or little change, unless something pushes them off course.

We can look back through history and see such strong examples of this regulatory behavior.

Many countries, many societies all creating neutrality in personality. It is as though living in fear of "different".

In actuality it could easily be fear that lead to the pattern of suppression of individuality of spirit.

Uniformity in thoughts is what has been used to control minds and behavior, to create robots in a sense.

Because something has been, does not make it good or right.

These wrongs were committed unintentionally, I am not pointing fingers and I do not want to focus on the negative side of the results. I feel very blessed to have all the examples that I have had in my life and to have the opportunity to know that there is a better and best yet.

The possibilities for this pattern are endless, but it is changing the precedent that is important.

It is the "Concept" that I want to focus on.

By creating a consciousness of the effects of current behavioral patterns and to suggest a shift in the awareness to a betterment of all.

To begin this change we need to begin at the source, as I have stated before. To recognize the divine beauty of each spirit, knowing they are on their own path in this life. In creating this life purpose support for our children, we will be able to also create the awareness in ourselves and both will recognize, develop and move in their own light of beauty and greatest good. Each individual's Divineness will be recognized.

Parents instilling in their children their right of unlimited thinking and creativity will have lasting effects.

Marilyn Louise Lawrence

Your kids require you most of all to love them
for who they are, not to spend your whole
time trying to correct them". Bill Ayers

I was talking with a dear friend of mine the other day
and she told me a story that so relates to this concept.
Her 6-year-old son Daniel was waiting in line for the
school bus behind a boy a couple of years older. From
the distance came a familiar sound to all and the older boy
spoke up, "here comes the bus". To which my friend's son
responded, "it might not be a school bus, it could be a
garbage truck". The debate between the two boys began.
"It couldn't be a garbage truck, the older boy retorted,
because garbage trucks are green". Daniel refuted, "they
could have painted it". "No", continued the older boy.
"Well why not, why couldn't they have painted it".

The parents were amused by the discussion. My
friend did not make any reaction to the stance that her
son took; whether she felt one way or another, she just
let him talk, voice his own expressions.

As my friend drove to work, she began recounting
the words that were exchanged and then was profoundly
moved.
Well why not?

Why couldn't they have painted the school bus?

The idea kept playing in her head. Limitless imagination was still alive in her sons mind; however the boy standing in front of him had shut down his creative side. Things were becoming matter of fact, black and white. It is with exchanges like this that children are influenced to second-guess their thoughts and words. If my friend had interjected in the conversation to correct her son, perhaps thinking she would be saving him from embarrassment, then doubt would have been magnified in Daniel, doubt in the fact that anything is possible, school buses can be painted.

Kudos to my friend for having the foresight not to step in and correct her son, but to instead allow him to use his unlimited imagination without correction. It is a simple step that helps support an individual's character. If every adult were to take this simple step a shift would occur. Soon enough the truth would make it self-visible, but until then, unrestricted thoughts would flourish. The creative mind could trigger an avalanche of possibilities. Self-doubt would not be present.

Chapter Four

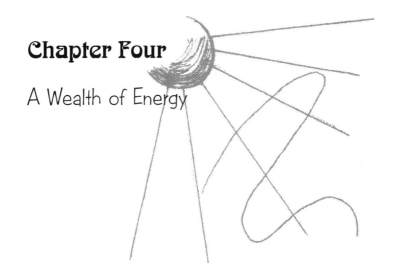

A Wealth of Energy

I have heard so many adults say, "My son/daughter, friend's child, niece, etc. has "too much energy".

I want to laugh aloud.

Too much energy? Is there such a thing?

The reality is that some of the greatest leaders and some of the most magnificent changes throughout history, have been made by people with "too much energy".

"We may not be able to prepare the future for our children, but we can at least prepare our children for the future". Franklin D. Roosevelt

Unfortunately, these same adults try to figure a way to change the child and stifle their energy. Making them feel badly about a valuable trait/gift they were born with. I say valuable because when these children are taught how to direct all their own energy, accomplishments are limitless.

The key is to realize that these children need direction. The parents of these children have been given the assignment of directing these special souls. These parents would not be gifted this task if they were not worthy and did not possess the ability to direct these children to their full potential.

If in fact you are a parent with a child of high energy, then you will need to quiet yourself and ask for the directions that you need to help this child reach their full potential. Know, without doubt, that you do have all the abilities, answers and guidance necessary. They have already been given to you and if you are not currently aware of them, they just need to be awakened. A combination of being born with all the tools you needed and your life experiences to date have prepared you for this event.

Sometimes the easiest way to awaken direction is by giving complete faith to every message you receive. Do not second-guess it, which is something that is so common, especially if you were shut down at a young age. Trust your inner voice, your gut feeling, your sixth sense. It is unfortunate that this ability has been shut down in so many, but obviously, there would be no reason for this book if every soul on earth were an enlightened one. We have to start sometime and today is a good day. After all, these children can make wonderful discoveries for all if allowed to do so.

If the truth were known, in the process of transforming to a more enlightened adult for the purpose of becoming the best guide for children, we are in fact already making a huge shift in the global knowingness and awareness.

Adults focusing on discovery of a better self, so they in turn can help children all around them with their gifted purpose will expand belief in divine limitless possibilities.

The balance of knowingness and doubt will be shifted. As doubt is lessened in the thoughts and souls of humans, then enlightenment will begin to shine brightly again.

It is encouraging and joyful for me to watch an interaction between a child and an adult that demonstrates an example to this age sensitive support. I say age sensitive, because there is a period in a child's life when they stop listening; stop believing and doubt and fear create the misguidance and misdirection that they are left with to operate on, as we have discussed early in this book. Thrown off their course and on to someone else's, trying desperately to fit in and make it work. Living someone else's dreams and patterns and confused why it does not feel right and why it is so difficult.

I had the honor of sitting with a few children I know, all aged 4 to 7 at the time. Each child sat with me individually in an effort to protect the child's privacy and help them feel completely comfortable to share their stories. I asked them the same questions and each question was asked twice, one time regarding current, present feelings of things and the second of their feelings from when they were young. I kept the questions simple and asked for thoughts, feedback and feelings from each child as we went along. What is your favorite color now, what was it when you were little and what do you want to do when you grow up, what did you want to do when you were little, are examples of some of the questions.

Remembering that these children were all close to, if not already in the cut off age range of remembering the life purpose they brought with them to this life. It was so intriguing that there was no hesitation when the children answered the questions. Interesting there was no hesitation in the children when I asked the questions about being younger. Each answered immediately. After I collected all the information and answers from the children, I asked what I thought to be a couple questions that are more difficult.

Why did you make the change in favorites was the first? These answers took a little longer. Interestingly enough and without exception, each child made mention of someone(s) that had influenced them to make the change. Most were made fun of by someone or made to feel like a baby or wrong for their own taste, likes and thoughts.

I had been gifted a clear example of the Concept to which I am referring and presenting.

"The wisest students are the teachers that learn from their own lessons". ML Lawrence

Ask any child when they are very young, ages under seven, what they want to be when they grow up and hold on to this information. It is very important information.

A child knows their purpose when they come in to this world. It is only when they grow older and become distracted with things that are not theirs that this information is lost. Sometimes it is never recovered, sometimes late in life this information is brought to light again and the truth of it makes perfect sense.

With this information, you are able to help your child on their life purpose path.

When I was five, I wanted to be a nurse, a teacher and a mom.

Chapter Five

Another Brilliant Example

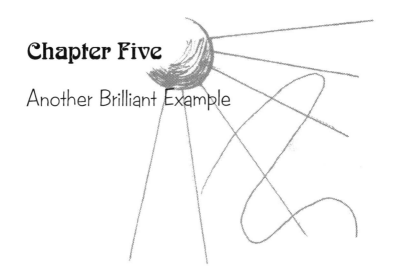

My son recently reminded me of a way of thinking that has again been receiving much international attention. He attended a lecture in which the professor discussed and showed a video of a study entitled "divergent thinking" as it related to children from kindergarten age to adulthood. Michael discussed the correlation of the principles with me and how they paralleled. Realizing how this information so brilliantly and preciously corresponded to the concept of uniformity in thinking that I had been writing about, he anxiously brought this thought process to my attention.

As I researched divergent thinking, I too was moved with the paradigm.

If you are not familiar with divergent thinking, I am providing you with some basic information for review and erudition.

The definition as shared via Wikipedia, the free encyclopedia:

Divergent thinking is a thought process or method used to generate creative ideas by exploring many possible solutions. It is often used in conjunction with convergent thinking, which follows a particular set of logical steps to arrive at one solution, which in some cases is a "correct" solution. Divergent thinking typically occurs in a spontaneous, free-flowing manner, such that many ideas are generated in an emergent cognitive fashion. Many possible solutions are explored in a short amount of time, and unexpected connections are drawn. After the process of divergent thinking has been completed, ideas and information are organized and structured using convergent thinking.[1]

Psychologists have found that a high IQ alone does not guarantee creativity. Instead, personality traits that promote divergent thinking are more important. Divergent thinking is found among people with personalities which have traits such as nonconformity, curiosity, willingness to take risks, and persistence.[2]

Additionally, researchers at Vanderbilt University found that musicians are more adept at utilizing both hemispheres and more likely to use divergent thinking in their thought processes.[3]

Activities which promote divergent thinking include creating lists of questions, setting aside time for thinking and meditation, brainstorming, subject mapping / "bubble mapping", keeping a journal, creating artwork, and free writing.[1] In free writing, a person will focus on one particular topic and write non-stop about it for a short period of time, in a stream of consciousness fashion.[1]

The following is from the web site of the United Kingdom Literacy Trust, November 6, 2005

From Glasgow, A conference in March, 2005, by the Scottish Book Trust,

I quote:

"Sir Ken Robinson, chair of the UK Government's report on creativity, education and the economy, described research that showed that young people lost their ability to think in "divergent or non-linear ways", a key component of creativity. Of 1,600 children aged three to five who were tested, 98% showed they could think in divergent ways. By the time they were aged eight to 10, 32% could think divergently. When the same test was applied to 13 to 15-year-olds, only 10% could think in this way. And when the test was used with 200,000 25-year-olds, only 2% could think divergently. . . . Education is driven by the idea of one answer and this idea of divergent thinking becomes stifled.' He described creativity as the 'genetic code' of education and said it was essential for the new economic circumstances of the 21st century." signed: (TESS, 25 March 2005) source - http://www. literacytrust.org.uk/Database/thinking.html#wither

Copyright © National Literacy Trust 2008 (UK)

The above quote is from 2005

My studies uncovered a plethora of individuals in many different careers and life patterns that embraced the concept of divergent thinking. I have included just a few of the sources, but the list is massive.

Divergent thinking highlights the fact that children, at a very young age, are instructed how to respond correctly to questions and how to correctly arrive at the "accepted" answer.

I am amazed by the information I have read and can only sit back and shake my head in wonderment. I say wonderment, because it is just that, wonderment that any souls break the molds of uniformity and homogeny.

First these beautiful golden souls are stripped of individual character in their very young life by family and friends and then they are sent to school where the current environment is one of streamlining and standardization.

I am again challenged to think of the brilliant leaps our society would and could make if individuals were nurtured and taught to respect the gifts that they brought with them to this world. Gifts that they were given to accomplish a purpose. A purpose that is divinely blessed.

Certainly convergent thinking will be necessary and sound at some points and in some situations, however basing education models on convergent thinking solely is desensitizing a person's abilities and full potential.

I am awe struck when I think of the possibilities of brilliant minds unfolding naturally, without criticism and without being shut-down.

If fear of not conforming were a non-issue, better yet, if conforming were the new "no".

If freedom in reaching one's full potential, freedom of creating a multitude of answers and responses and freedom of being one's true golden gift to the world were embraced whole-heartedly, what possibilities would and could be had by all.

It truly is an awe-inspiring idea. A collaborative effort between all parties involved in the influence of new souls based on the intellectually superior idea that these golden souls will flourish if care and attention is given to their individual gift to the world. Society based conformity, fear of not fitting in and rejection, fear of being different, will become antiquated idealisms and memories of a past and society gone astray.

Chapter Six

A Few More Messages

I have been on such an incredible observation path.

Actually, it seems I have been observing the same, but learning more from my observations... that is a better way to put it.

When I observe a person's reaction and then examine the possible reasons behind the reaction, my own reactions to things become illuminated.

As an example, I was confused as to why a certain couple of people "got under my skin" so to speak. Why their actions bothered me and not only bothered me, but stayed with me. For days, I would replay the incident(s) looking for clarity, second thinking my reaction to an event, frustrated with myself for letting it bother me so much, a whole gamete of emotions swirling around something that should have been forgotten immediately. More than likely I thought the second party to this had forgotten the event and perhaps had not even given it a second thought. Why then was I so transfixed on it? Obsessed in some cases.

I was gifted the simple answer, "if you cannot make sense of something, then it is not yours".

Have you ever said to yourself, "I can't believe I just said that", or "that's not like me"? Then it is not you.

You have taken on someone else's energy, (stuff) unknowingly.

It is time to sit and clear whatever it is that you are "carrying" of someone else's. You do not need to know what it is or who it is; you just need to make a conscience effort to clear anything and everything you are carrying that is not yours. It is not your responsibility to carry it, it will do you absolutely no good, and in most cases, it will weigh you down and keep you in a confused state, which is not good.

The sooner that people pay attention and realize this and release the better.

In another example, I had been confused with a friendship that had been very strong when I was going through difficult times in my life, but when things were good for me, the friendship seemed to falter and become problematic.

Some people rise to the occasion when someone is down. They become a knight in shining armor or a Florence Nightingale, devoted to the person that is suffering.

However, when things change for the suffering person and they become better, start succeeding and exceeding, that same friend changes. It is as though they cannot handle the success or betterment of the other person.

This behavior has become quite clear to me now from the message that I received. It is no fault of either person.

As I said earlier, "people do not know what they do not know".

If someone does not know the energy of abundance for example, then they cannot relate to it. On the other hand, if they know the energy of poverty, then they will seek that emotional equal. People seek what they know, because it is more comforting, less resistant, it is all they know at the time. The basic law of attraction, like attracts like. Therefore, the people that are so wonderful to you when you are down, know the feeling or energy of suffering, of poverty, failure, depression, defeated, the list goes on. However, once a "cared for" changes their energy vibration and begin pulling in hope, happiness, success, abundance, positive energies, the caregiver may not be able to relate to the new energy and begins to feel threatened, unsure of what happened, they become competitive or angry, shifting the whole personality of the relationship. Both sides are left feeling confused as to why the relationship has declined or worse dissolved.

Many times when people are going through difficult times, they are surrounded by drama / chaotic energy vibrations. Because all of their attention is given to resolving the problem, most are not aware that they have and are "wearing" these vibrations. Depending on the length of time that people are involved with a problem, they could become very familiar with the feeling of drama and chaos and when the problem is solved, they unintentionally seek a situation to continue the same energy. They begin "wearing" these negative energies and therefore attracting the same kind of energy and people with the same energy creating a snowball effect, in some cases spiraling out of control. It is not until they step back and seek an answer to the events that this is brought to light. The answer could be clear to them once they have stepped back, it could come from a friend, it could come from reading a book and sometimes sadly, it may not come at all.

I am sure that you can quickly recall examples of both, especially in today's economic environment, the number of people who have lost or are losing their homes and then others that have been able to keep them.

People need to pay attention and not continue the "need" or "feeding" on negative energy such as drama.

If you feel you are on this path or know someone that is, take a close look at your life and the people in it. If you are not enjoying something, look at the character of each action. Look at each friend you are close with. Determine what energies you have in common and then determine which need to be modified to create the life and person you want to be.

This must be done from a non-judgmental place with a pure heart. Everyone is on their own path. You are the master of putting and keeping yourself on your true-life purpose path, just as those around you are responsible for their own. Not everyone is learning the same lessons in this life and not everyone has the same path to their purpose. Understand that you are not letting anyone down by choosing a different direction. You are instead honoring the purpose gifted to you at birth.

By creating a better awareness for yourself, you are awarding others, by example, the opportunity to create their own better self and awaken their gifted life purpose.

We all need to begin now to change our focus and our frequency.

We can make a difference.
What We do Matters!

Chapter Seven

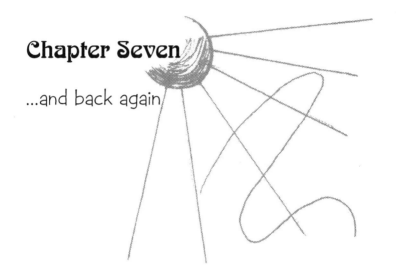

...and back again

As I hung up the phone with Brandon I realized that he was right, my book did an excellent job of bringing to light the importance of devoting attention to the children that have been entrusted to us, but something was missing. What about the adults wanting to make the discovery of their own truth?

Everyone has a "Truth of Being".

As I have ascertained in my conversations with every adult I have spoken to about my book, regarding the importance of our dedication to a child's purpose, it was not the child's interest that came to the adults minds first, but rather their own. Without exception every adult agreed to the importance of "The Concept" and then were taken back immediately to their own childhoods. Stories of how their parents, aunts, cousins, etc. had affected their free right of expression and pursuit of purpose. Being shut down was a vivid memory to all that I have spoken with.

It was not just the child's golden soul and right of pursuit and support to life purpose that needs attention;

it is every person, young and old that needs help in awakening their own Truth.

It was as though I could hear the inner child in each of these adults waking up and crying out for help. Recognizing that they could once again realize their Divine path; the path that was selected for them, by them. These dreams and devotions hidden so long ago under layers of scars, fears, hurts and anger were again possible. A bright light was being shown deep inside their souls opening a tunnel to release their unlimited possibilities.

A new discovery was possible, the discovery of their own life's purpose, their own
"Truth of Being".

But where to start?

The best place to start is right here,
right now.

The following pages contain step by step tools that I have developed to help with the awakening to purpose process.

This may be as quick or as slow an evolution as you would like. Remember we all possess the ability of manifestation.

If you Believe It, Then It Is.
If you Think It, Then It Is.
If you Dream It, Then It Is.
If you think it cannot be, Then It Is.

Be acutely aware of your thoughts, because your thoughts will direct you forward, backward or keep you stagnant. Do not ever limit yourself, because you are capable of feats that have yet to be discovered, trails that have yet to be forged and miracles that are waiting for you to make reality.

I have full Faith in you and You should never have anything less!

Rekindling the Fire To Pursue Your Life Purpose Path

The following exercises are for you and you alone. You do not have to share this information with anyone, or you may share it with everyone. You are in control of "you" again. Take back your courage. Begin to recognize again that "steering voice" inside of you, your "gut feeling". Trust yourself and let go of fear and doubt. The more you program yourself to trust your feelings the faster things will manifest for you.

We have been programmed as a society to live in fear and doubt; it all goes back to what I spoke of earlier in the book. As a very young child you believed in yourself, you had no reason not to. You were born with the perfect operating system to pursue your purpose, that was until you were taught to doubt yourself by others around you. You have the right to reclaim your voice.

Reclaim your own truth.

From this day forward no one else has the right to steer you off course. You do possess all you need; you do have the courage to discover your Gifts. You are a special soul gifted to this earth for a special reason.

Let's discover what that is, shall we?

Take time to complete the following questions and statements. You may find as you go along you will add more to each.

Remember you are removing the layers that are hiding "You". It may take longer for some as I said, depending on how hidden you have kept yourself, coupled with how much Permission and Faith you give yourself and your answers. This is for you. There are no right and wrong answers. You are the boss of you.

Another important thing to practice as you move through these tools of remembering you, is to not over think the process. Often times one will get an answer to something and then start thinking about the answer, analyzing it, rethinking it and pretty soon you doubt the answer that was given to you. You need to know that you can trust yourself and the answers that are coming to you. Once you get a message, believe it and write it down. Do not doubt, do not second guess, just believe and move forward. The more you practice this, the easier the process will become for you and you will be amazed at how much you are able to uncover.

Let's begin.

Think back to when you were a child age 1 to age 5. At some point, by someone you were asked what you wanted to be when you grew up. It could be when you were in playschool, kindergarten, first grade. Think hard, because every child has this information. A teacher may have asked the class, an adult may have asked you, at some point you were tasked to remember what you slated as your direction when you entered this world. At this age there is nothing that causes doubt or second thinking. Everything is a positive. Everything can be done; in fact the thought of something not being done does not compute or enter into a child's field.

At age four I wanted to be a Nurse, a Teacher and a Mom. Information I had hidden until I dedicated myself to this Concept. Interestingly enough as I look at those three aspirations I am gifted with the fact of how much I have stayed on this path.

Following is your first question. Again do not over think. Write what comes to you without analyzing it. These are your truths and they will ring out clearly when you close the left brain thinker and let the information just come to you. List as many as you can think of. If it is just one, then so be it. You can also add to this list if more details come to you later.

1). What did you want to be when you Grew Up? "Your Child List"

_____

_____

_____

_____

_____

_____

_____

_____

_____

_____

_____

_____

_____

_____

_____

_____

_____

2). What external influences affected the pursuit of your Child List?

Take time here and list everything you can think of, small and large. Memories may come to you slowly at first and then like a flood. However they do, list everything and everyone that you think of. Do not over think this step. Do not analyze your answers or the process. Just let things flow out, release everything you can think and feel on the pages below.

This process may stir up emotions, in fact more than likely it will. You have been wounded in essence and we are getting to the core of the wound so that you may begin to heal and regain your own focus.

Many people may need more space than is provided for you here. Release as much as comes up over a period of hours, days and months. You owe yourself this time of releasing and healing. Call on the Angels for help. They are here to help everyone that calls on them.

_____

_____

_____

_____

_____

_____

_____

_____

_____

_____

Marilyn Louise Lawrence

It is imperative in the last exercise that you do not lay blame on yourself or anyone else. Firstly, that will do no good, but instead will hide the path of clear visualization of purpose. Whatever happened to keep you off track happened; it just is.

You cannot blame yourself; you did not have the full awareness until now. You cannot blame anyone else; they did not know the difference or have the awareness.

We together are making a shift in consciousness.

There will be emotions stimulated as you process your responses. That is wonderful, as you will be given an indicator light if you will, that shows you what you are doing is working. You are removing layers to find yourself. Keep up the good work!

The purpose of this is to help you remember what it is you were born to do, uncover your "Truth of Being".

Once you realize what your Truth is and are aware of what has prevented you from keeping it your focus, then you will have a knowingness that you will never again loose. In fact, you will never again want to lose it. You will experience such a massive sense of Truth and Pure Joy when you discover your purpose that you will not want to ignore it again.

3). What internal influences affected the pursuit of your Child List?

_____

_____

_____

_____

_____

_____

_____

_____

_____

_____

_____

_____

_____

_____

_____

_____

_____

_____

_____

_____

_____

_____

_____

_____

4). Have you accomplished or begun to accomplish your goals of #1?

If so, in what ways?

If not, what has prevented you?

_____

_____

_____

_____

_____

_____

_____

_____

_____

_____

_____

_____

_____

_____

_____

_____

_____

_____

_____

_____

_____

_____

_____

Marilyn Louise Lawrence

(#4 continued)

_____
_____
_____
_____
_____
_____
_____
_____
_____
_____
_____
_____
_____
_____
_____
_____
_____
_____
_____
_____
_____
_____
_____
_____
_____
_____

Keep in mind that if you listed a doctor for instance, in #1, that is part of the healing path. You may not be a doctor by formal definition, but you may have studied or want to study massage, physical therapy, etc. Healing comes in many ways. It could be that you are helping a new author publish their first book and helping them walk through the path of obstacles undaunted; healing their path so to speak. Think beyond the obvious. Recognize the good you are doing now. Open yourself up to adding more options to incorporate your desires.

If you have discovered that nothing you are currently doing can be related in any way to your "child list", then you have been gifted an awareness too. This could be why you are so unhappy with your job/career. Why you are always feeling like you are searching for something you cannot find; as though Joy is eluding you. When you are doing your purpose then you will be surrounded by Joy and Truth.

I should mention now that I am in no means suggesting you quit your job or change your environment immediately. What I am saying is, you have been "re-gifted" information that your soul recognizes as truth. You will now be searching out ways to align yourself with the direction that you know is your Life Path; your "Truth of Being".

Your energy has shifted just by reading this. You now have a knowingness. You will now begin focusing on your purpose either intentionally or unintentionally at first. As many brilliant minds have proven, once you begin thinking about something, putting intention behind your thoughts, you are creating energy awareness. Since like energies attract, you will begin drawing energies to you that will set you on your path. Be aware that sometimes this happens gradually and sometimes it happens with a jolt. Whichever the case, it is a wonderfully freeing and blessed thing!

The more intention you put behind something, the faster you will be able to manifest it.

I remember clearly the first time life purpose was placed in my thinking. I was having a body treatment at a beautiful salon in Orange County, CA. At the end of the treatment the therapist told me about a book she had written and the focus of her work. Then she asked if she could say a prayer for me. Of course I agreed. She took my hands and prayed that I would be given the awareness of my life purpose and be given help in my pursuit. I went along my way, not thinking much about it, but being very appreciative that someone would take the time to ask that favor for me.

It wasn't until a couple of years ago I remembered that event and the frenzy of the prior four years were put to reason. I had experienced a sequence of (at that time) unexplainable events that jetted me on the path that I am now. Once I asked to be shown my life purpose a shift was made and when I committed myself to it, my life has not been the same.

This is an example of a timeframe, my timeframe. I was shown an awareness that there was such a thing as a life purpose, however I did not have the awareness that I had a purpose independent of everyone else; that every person is gifted a special path at birth. I had to stumble around for a bit until I saw these things clearly. Until I paid attention to the messages that were being sent to me. I am hoping with the information in this book that you will have a quicker path to your happiness. From this day forward I want you to Pay Attention to all the signs and messages that are being sent to you. The sooner you listen and observe, the better the course.

I thank God and the Angels every day for my wonderful happy life.

Please understand that I am not making religious rights here, I do believe in God and thank Him and the Angels every morning when I wake up and every night when I go to bed. I talk with Jesus, Mother Mary, the Ascended Masters and my Guides for clarity and help. I am very thankful for all that I have been shown and have been given. I am thankful that my eyes have been opened up to limitless possibilities. I work hard every day to speak from a place of pure love and truth.

I know, without exception, that when you focus on your Purpose all else will fall in to place.

I feel the Joy of Divine Purpose.

These are things that I wish for everyone, no matter what their religious affiliation.

4). Applying the Information that you have gathered.

Now that you have awakened your mind and soul to the search of your infinite possibilities in exercise one and have begun to establish why and when you moved off course in exercise two, three and four, it is time to figure out how to get back in your gifted flow of life.

Quite honestly, as I referenced above, you have already created a shift and have sent "the memo" that it is "Time" by your interest and willingness to read and embrace this information. Your energy has changed so you will begin receiving information and opportunities to help you. Remember to pay attention to these messages. It could be someone new that you meet, it could be that you begin changing your current friend group to eliminate drama and distraction, things will begin happening for you. Take everything as a gift with full knowingness that you are being helped.

Do not react to any shifts in a negative way. You have asked for help, so receive everything with positive energy. If you respond negatively, then you are sending out a message that you are not ready, are not committed, etc. Pay close attention to this. Receive humbly with open arms as you are being gifted "You".

If you are not currently on a path that compliments your child path then it is time to begin the journey.

Only you will know the right way to proceed after hearing the messages that are being sent to you and shown to you.

It is wise to have a calculated approach, but again this is only my opinion. In calculated approach I am meaning a game plan.

Especially true if this change is something like a job that will affect you with negative consequences. In cases like this it is wise to have tactical steps to making the change. Of course the first step is stating with intention that you would like a job doing...or in the ...field, etc. Put the energy out that you want something so that it will come to you. Do this with intention.

1). What do I want?

_____
_____
_____
_____
_____
_____
_____
_____
_____
_____
_____
_____
_____
_____
_____
_____
_____
_____
_____
_____
_____
_____
_____
_____
_____
_____

2). How am I going to achieve it?

_____

_____

_____

_____

_____

_____

_____

_____

_____

_____

_____

_____

_____

_____

_____

_____

_____

_____

_____

_____

_____

_____

_____

_____

3). What resistance am I going to face with these actions?

_____

_____

_____

_____

_____

_____

_____

_____

_____

_____

_____

_____

_____

_____

_____

_____

_____

_____

_____

_____

_____

_____

_____

_____

4). Who am I going to affect with these actions?

_____

_____

_____

_____

_____

_____

_____

_____

_____

_____

_____

_____

_____

_____

_____

_____

_____

_____

_____

_____

_____

_____

5). How can I accomplish my goals without any negative effects from any of the above answers?

_____

_____

_____

_____

_____

_____

_____

_____

_____

_____

_____

_____

_____

_____

_____

_____

_____

_____

_____

_____

_____

Another ancient tool that is extremely effective at shifting energy and helping with manifesting is chanting. Chanting is used universally for a variety of different reasons from religious practices, sports contests, football chants, battle cries, auction cries, music scores and even movies. All of which is a practice of repeating something over and over, generally in a rhythmic tone.

I was introduced to this tool at one of the many classes my husband and I have taken from Melinda Hess, an incredibly talented clairvoyant and a decidedly educated universal healer.

It is a very simple and highly effective technique of changing thought patterns.

The key is to determine what it is that you wish to begin accomplishing, feeling, producing, etc. and then choosing the words that make sense to you when you say them.

As you are lying in bed, before falling asleep, repeat your chant over and over in your head. Not only will you have the huge benefit of quieting your thoughts from the day, but you will begin focusing on the things that you really want for yourself and of yourself.

The thoughts you have before you fall asleep are very important. They set the tone for your dreams and also the tone for when you wake, therefore the pattern of your life. Make sure that the thoughts you have are ones that you want to live with. Thinking about the problems at work, drama with friends, arguments that you have had will program that negative energy into your being.

If you can do one useful thing for yourself tonight, make this be it. Tell yourself good positive things. Chant positive until you fall asleep. Either aloud or to yourself, both ways work.

This is another case where you should not over think. Do not let your thoughts complicate the message that you receive. Simply ask yourself what you want to focus on at the time, then ask for the words that feel right to say and put them together in a chant that feels comfortable and rings with truth.

Use this same chant for a minimum of one month.

My chant contains just 4 words that I repeat over and over until I drift to sleep.

I have used the same chant for nearly 2 years.

Chapter Eight

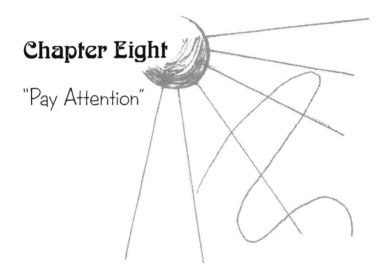

"Pay Attention"

The Concept that I am bringing to light with this book is certainly to arouse and heighten our skills with helping the children around us.

The Concept Awakens *Your* Truth and reminds you to focus on the
You that you were born to be.

It teaches you that every person has their own path, not for you to judge or be envious of, but rather to embrace and support and learn from as others will learn from you.

Believe in your Truth. When you have thoughts sneak in like the "what if's", (what if it doesn't work, what if people don't get it, what if I get negative feedback, etc.) remember that you believe in your truth. You have sent out to the universe the memo that you are opening up your life purpose path and truth of being. Do not doubt the messages that come to you in your pursuit. Maintain full faith at all times. Ask for clearer messages if need be, clearer directions, but do not doubt yourself.

Fear will keep you stagnant, confused, and distracted or even move you backyards. Immerse yourself in the full faith of your Divine purpose and then

"PAY ATTENTION" !

Pay Attention to children when they are born and at very young ages, because they will be able to remember and tell you what their path in life is.

Pay Attention to the Divine beauty of each spirit. Tell children from birth "I believe in you and support you and your purpose".

Pay Attention to creating a consciousness to the effects of current behavioral patterns and to suggest a shift in the awareness to a betterment of all.

Pay Attention
Instead of saying to children (and to yourself) that you can do anything you want or choose to do, say "I believe in you and support you and your life purpose"; "you can be true to your life purpose"; "I have Faith in your life purpose"; "I believe in your life path", or any combination of these. In telling a child that they can do anything they want to do, though delivered with every good intention, in actuality puts a lot of pressure on anyone as the choices then are limitless. How can you decide on the best one or any ones for that matter. However, if you tell anyone that you believe

and support their life purpose, then it rings Truth to the one delivering the message as well as the recipient.

Pay Attention to embrace every person's purpose and not to create doubt, tease or steer and direct.

Pay Attention to the fact that you do have all the information needed for your life, and you are simply awakening what you know.

Pay Attention to the fact that until you know something, you do not know it, and the same is true with others.

Pay Attention to keep fear at bay.

Pay Attention to steer clear of drama and chaos as best you can.

Pay Attention to messages you receive everywhere you are.

Once you begin doing this you will become better and better and then you will even be able to see the humor in some of your messages. The Angels have a wonderful sense of humor. They remind us to lighten things up and enjoy. I have found when I experience a random event that I heed special attention and look even closer for the message.

Pay Attention that you are opening up opportunities for yourself, others and children, but do not direct the actions or push. Accept the gifts given to you in the form of ideas and opportunities. There can only be one captain and each person is the captain of their path.

Pay Attention not to put limits on yourself. You do have the ability to manifest greatness beyond your wildest imagination. You have sent the message out to the universe. Allow it to unfold the way it needs to. Do not under estimate or put limits on your outcome. Do not expect a pebble when you could have mountains.

Pay Attention not to let fear or doubt stop you. It comes in many forms and will surprise you at different times. Just remember it is not welcome anymore.

If you stop yourself because you tell yourself "someone has already done this, or said this, or written this" then you need to remember you would not have been given the information if it was not important. You have opened up to your purpose so the message, task, assignment needs to be done. Do not second guess why. If anyone reacts negatively, simply remember that it is not their message to hear. There will be plenty that your message is meant for and leave it at that.

You have asked for help and have been given it.

As I always say, do not send something out to God, the Angels and the universe asking for help and then take it back and mess with it, then send it back out, then take it back and mess with it in a revolving cycle. You have asked for help, it will come, have Faith.

Pay Attention to the fact that not everyone is learning the same lessons in this life and not everyone has the same path to their purpose. Show respect.

Pay Attention that you approach everyone and every situation with a Pure Loving heart. When doing so, you will receive the same.

Realizing every person is born with a special life purpose is of key importance. If you are lucky enough to begin utilizing this Concept with a young soul around you, then what a blessing you have been given. You will be able to guide a soul and get yourself back on track, reawakening your purpose, at the same time.

Perhaps you have this time to focus on your own rebirth and recognition of your life purpose. Whatever the case, this book has gifted you with an awareness that is now a knowingness of a Concept that will aid you in the discovery of your own truth.

After all...

It is never too late to go from
Blue back to Pink!

Credits

Melinda Hess
www.melindahesspsychic.com

http://www.goodreads.com/quotes/
show_tag?id=children

http://www.literacytrust.org.uk/
Database/thinking.html#wither
Copyright © National Literacy Trust 2008 (UK)

Wikipedia

Children are born with it; most adults have long forgotten it. Now is the time to reawaken your "Truth of Being" and Life Purpose. *From Pink to Blue* is a divinely guided message initially designed to enlighten the purpose path of children by creating a knowingness, awareness, and concept in the adults around them.

Much to the author's surprise, this concept deeply touches the very essence of purpose and awakens a truth, not only in children but in every person who reads these words, including herself.

This truth has been hidden deep inside, shut down, suppressed and closed in a dark room since a young age, when one felt a need to protect oneself based on the words and actions of others.

In this book, you will learn that helping a child with a life purpose path is just the beginning of what can be accomplished.

The time is now for awakening the injured child inside of people, so the healing process can begin for the betterment of all.

Throughout her life, Marilyn Lawrence knew that there was a special purpose for her, but being a single mom and focusing on a busy career, she lost sight of her path. Then a series of unavoidable, undeniable experiences gave her the message loud and clear and made it difficult to avoid her purpose any longer. A spiritual author and teacher, Marilyn's work is grounded in the strong belief that every person has been placed in this world with a special "divine gift" to share and a purpose to guide them. With Marilyn's passionate commitment to spiritual service through classes, retreats, personal readings, and healings, she has helped many people remove obstacles in their lives so they can once again feel the infinite joy of their own purpose.